Original title:
The Ocean's Crystal Heart

Copyright © 2025 Creative Arts Management OÜ
All rights reserved.

Author: Wyatt Kensington
ISBN HARDBACK: 978-1-80587-444-7
ISBN PAPERBACK: 978-1-80587-914-5

Phantoms in the Deep

Beneath the waves, a swirling dance,
Fish in tuxedos, taking a chance.
Octopuses juggling, what a delight,
Seaweed confetti, it's quite a sight!

Starfish in sandals, they waddle around,
Laughing at crabs with their sideways bound.
A dolphin's joke, oh how it soars,
Tickling the turtles on sandy shores.

Sharks in a chorus, singing off-key,
Bubbles of laughter, as bright as can be.
A sea cucumber throws a fit,
"Why can't I dance? I don't have a bit!"

Clams in a row, don't want to be caught,
Playing hide and seek, they are so distraught.
A treasure chest grins, with coins that will gleam,
In this wacky world, it's all just a dream!

Seashell Lullabies

In the sand, a shell hums,
Singing tunes of ocean drums.
A crab joins in, with a little dance,
While a fish says, "Give me a chance!"

Waves clap their hands, spry and bright,
A dolphin's laugh echoes in flight.
Seashells giggle, they're quite the sight,
As starfish spin with pure delight!

Kaleidoscope of the Depths

A jellyfish floats with a funny grace,
While seaweed's doing the twist in place.
Turtles wear shades, oh what a trend!
And seahorses giggle, they just can't pretend!

Fish dart past in rainbow hues,
Sharing jokes like morning news.
An octopus winks, says, "Can I join?"
While crabs play marbles with pebbles, just coin!

Brushed by the Sea Breeze

The wind whispers tales of playful tricks,
As seagulls tease with their acrobatic kicks.
A seal cracks jokes that echo and roll,
While a sandpiper dances, it's on a stroll!

Beach balls bounce with a giggling sound,
As children run and jump all around.
Laughter like bubbles floats in the air,
As a starfish shouts, "Hey, look, I'm rare!"

Luminescent Depths

In twilight's glow, the squid does a jig,
While plankton twirl, feeling quite big.
A pufferfish puffs, trying on flair,
Giggling at eels with wild, frizzy hair!

Anglerfish grins in neon light,
Says, "What's cooking? Join me for a bite!"
A sea cucumber slides by with a sigh,
"Life's just a party, oh my, oh my!"

Shimmering Depths

Bubbles rise like giggles bright,
Fish in tuxedos, what a sight!
Seaweed dances, all so grand,
Shaking fins, a wobbly band.

Waves tease crabs, oh what a game,
Clams get sassy, that's their fame.
Starfish cheer, they can't stay still,
Flipping over with their thrill.

Waves of Whispered Dreams

Seagulls gossip, plot and scheme,
Rolling waves disrupt their dream.
Sandy towels turn into ships,
While sunscreen dances on our lips.

Jellyfish boogie, float with flair,
Octopuses brush 'dos with care.
Salty snacks gone in a whirl,
As shells giggle, join the twirl.

Liquid Infinity

Splashing puddles, oh what fun,
Chasing fish, but they all run!
Mermaids laugh, they take a dive,
Winks and splashes, truly alive.

Giant squids, they tell tall tales,
While shrimps on scooters zoom like snails.
Coral reefs host wild parades,
Dancing sea cucumbers in spades.

Heart of the Abyss

Deep down below where no one goes,
Silly fish wear funny clothes.
A whale sings in a goofy tone,
Echoes of laughter, never alone.

Crabs throw parties, snap their claws,
Shouting jokes, the crowd, it roars.
Underwater tickles, quite absurd,
A world where silence is unheard.

Beneath the Surface: A Hidden Realm

Deep below, fish wear bowties,
Dancing around, oh what a surprise.
Octopuses juggle, seaweed the props,
While seahorses trot in fancy flip-flops.

Crabs in a conga, all on parade,
In this quirky place, there's no charade.
Turtles in top hats, moving so slow,
Waving to whales, who steal the show.

Waves of Ethereal Murmurs

Waves crash like laughter, bubbles take flight,
Mermaids trade gossip, oh what a sight!
Seashells are phones, ringing all day,
Telling tall tales of fish gone astray.

Sandy toes tap to the rhythm of tide,
Starfish sing karaoke, a smile wide.
Dolphins debate whose jump is the best,
In a splashy showdown, they never rest.

Liquid Jewels of the Blue Horizon

Rainbows of jelly, a floaty delight,
They giggle and wiggle, a colorful sight.
Pearls tell secrets, while corals just sigh,
And seagulls join in for a dance in the sky.

Bubbles that tickle, tickly and fun,
Bathing in laughter, they sparkle like sun.
Fish trade their fins for some glittery gear,
A flamboyant parade, let's give them a cheer!

A Voyage into Aquamarine Whispers

Sail away on a pineapple boat,
With kelp for sails, it'll stay afloat.
Gill-bert the fish, the captain so spry,
Riding the waves with a wink in his eye.

Crustaceans in capes, they zoom to the shore,
They giggle and wiggle, always asking for more.
With sea cucumbers playing the flute,
This oceanic party, oh what a hoot!

Secrets of the Salty Veil

Bubbles wiggle, fish do dance,
Seagulls squawk and steal a glance.
Waves are laughing, tides are bright,
Crabs in top hats, quite a sight!

Shells are gossiping on the shore,
Whispering tales of ocean lore.
A dolphin pranks with a playful spin,
While octopuses wave their fin!

Starfish share their fashion tips,
As seaweed sways and gently flips.
Mermaids giggle, flipping hair,
Spouting jokes—beyond compare!

Underwater, life's a jest,
Who knew bubbles could cause unrest?
With sandy jokes and salt spray cheer,
This hidden realm is full of cheer!

Coral Reverie

Coral castles sit in glee,
Home to fish with fancy tea.
A lobster wears a pirate hat,
While jellyfish float like a diplomat!

Seahorses skate in a grand ballet,
As clam bands start to play all day.
Turtles trot with fancy strut,
Who knew they'd be such silly mutts?

Anemones wave like they're on sale,
While anglerfish tell goofy tales.
With each wave, more laughter spreads,
Under the sea, there's no dread!

Crabs play cards in a sandy nook,
Arguing who's the best cook.
In this world, all worries wane,
Just ride the tide, let joy remain!

Shards of Pearlescent Light

Pearls are plucked from clammy friends,
Each one shines, but who pretends?
Caught in the tide, mischievous glee,
As starfish stretch for the cup of tea!

A sea turtle tells a pun so bad,
Waves crash softly, making them glad.
Fish in bow ties swim with zest,
In this water world, they jest!

Rainbow fish turn with a twirl,
In shimmering hues, they dance and swirl.
The squid serves up a noodle feast,
While crabs argue who's the least!

Each bubble bursts with a laugh aloud,
The guardians of the sea so proud.
From dawn till dusk, this light so bright,
Brings laughter from morning till night!

Fluid Harmony

Waves upon waves in rhythmic laugh,
Surfers yell, "Look at my craft!"
Barnacles play on the pier's edge,
While starfish argue who can hedge!

Snorkelers giggle, splashing about,
As the fish sneak in for a shout.
Dolphins do tricks with twist and spin,
While whale sings softly, inviting a grin!

Kelp dances softly, swaying wide,
As crabs join in for a wonky ride.
With wagging tails and fins that flip,
Life is a party on this salty trip!

Under the waves, there's so much cheer,
Every bubble a tale to share here.
Together we create pure delight,
In this funny world of blue and bright!

Dreamscapes in Blue

Bubbles rise and fish can dance,
In a sea of dreams, they prance.
Seahorses wear tiny shoes,
While jellyfish serenade the blues.

Crabs play poker on the sand,
With shells and seaweed in their hand.
Starfish beat a drum with glee,
Underwater parties full of spree.

Mermaids gossip with the waves,
Telling tales of silly knaves.
Octopuses paint with flair,
Making murals in the salty air.

Turtles race on surfboard rides,
As dolphins cheer for the high tides.
In this realm, life's a swim,
With laughter echoing everywhere, not grim.

Oceanic Serenade

Whales compose a symphony,
With bubbles bursting, oh so free.
Clowns in gills and a fishy joke,
They giggle where the guppy folks poke.

A starfish wears a cowboy hat,
While sea cucumbers dance like a brat.
Shrimps wear bling, they're dressing classy,
Boogie in the currents, feeling sassy.

Cranky crabs in a dance-off fight,
Whirling under flickering moonlight.
Seaweed sways to the beat onboard,
Making waves in a funky accord.

Clams gather 'round for a shanty sung,
With sea urchins strumming strings unsprung.
"Let's put on a show!" they chime and roar,
In this salty club, who could ask for more?

The Soul of the Sea

A fish with glasses reads the news,
While dolphins surf in vibrant hues.
Crabs debate the best sea snacks,
While sea turtles plan mischief tracks.

Seahorses zoom on underwater bikes,
With octopuses pulling pranks from spikes.
Coral reefs with laughter spill,
As clownfish dance on rubber gill.

Giant squids write poems at night,
With ink that glimmers, oh what a sight!
Stingrays glide in a disco ball,
Flipping and flopping, having a ball.

Fiddler crabs strut in a parade,
With a conch shell grand for their crusade.
Under the waves, the giggles soar,
In a bubbly world, laughter galore!

Ethereal Waters

In the deep, a fish does sing,
As shrimp take flight on fancy wings.
Whales wear hats made of sea foam,
In this watery world, they feel at home.

Clams do twirls in their pearly shells,
While jellyfish cast magical spells.
Turtles try to breakdance too,
But end up rolling—oh boo-hoo!

Dolphins leap with comedic flair,
Performing tricks in mid-air.
Sea stars giggle at the show,
As crabs applaud with a friendly glow.

Anemones wave like they're on stage,
While fish show off their cartoon age.
In this realm of whimsy and mirth,
Laughter bubbles through the ocean's girth.

Chasing Seafoam

I ran along the sandy edge,
With seafoam tickling my toes.
A wave gave chase, like a sly hedge,
And splashed my pants—oh, how it grows!

My laughter echoed with the breeze,
As seagulls cawed a silly tune.
I dodged and ducked with utmost ease,
While counting starfish by the moon.

Tranquil Depths

Beneath the waves, fish play charades,
In their bright costumes, they all prance.
Octopuses doing renegades,
As crabs attempt to join the dance.

Anemones like fluffy mobs,
Wave hi to everyone who floats.
While jellyfish, in fancy gobs,
Giggle in their translucent coats.

A Palette of Waves

The waves roll in, like a painter's brush,
Splattering white like a frothy dish.
Seashells are treasures, oh what a rush,
My bucket's filling—catching a wish!

The sandcastles rise like soggy dreams,
With moats and flags so wild and free.
But wait! Here comes an oddball's beams,
A wave that shouts, 'Come play with me!'

Luminescent Secrets

At night the sea glows, a disco ball,
With fish in tuxedos, they softly waltz.
A clam yelled 'boo!' and started to sprawl,
While starfish giggle, 'Don't fault our faults!'

Glowing plankton light up the show,
As waves crash down in rhythmic glee.
The moon joins in, a shimmering glow,
In the party of waves—what fun to be!

Beneath the Surface

Bubbles pop and fishy laugh,
A seal's attempt at a comedy craft.
Starfish star in their own way,
While clam shells clap at the fish ballet.

Turtles tell jokes, very slow,
While dolphins surf on waves, whoa!
Octopus plays puppet games,
With eight hands, it conquers fame!

Kelp wiggles in a jolly groove,
As crabs bust a move to a funky groove.
The seaweed's dance, a swirly sight,
In this underwater party, all feels right.

So bring your goggles, let's go play,
In the salty splash, we'll waltz all day.
With every giggle, the sea gives cheer,
Beneath the waves, we're free of fear!

Gemstone Waves

Waves of turquoise, rolling in,
A fish in shades of pink, with a grin.
Laughing corals giggle bright,
As pearls pop out, what a delight!

Sandy shores tell puns so grand,
From sea-glass shards to the happy sand.
A crab with shades strikes a pose,
While mermaids tease with their jelly toes.

Shells narrate tales of love lost,
Counting the laughs is never a cost.
The starry night glimmers on the bay,
As fishy friends rhyme the night away.

So grab your nets and throw away strife,
We'll dance on waves for the rest of our life.
With sparkling humor in salty air,
Each tide brings laughs, no need to share.

Chromatic Currents

Rainbow fish parade in style,
With colorful fins that make us smile.
Jellyfish disco, glowing bright,
In the party of waves, hearts take flight.

Seahorses ride, looking so cool,
While turtles float like they rule the pool.
With a flip and a flop, they breakdance too,
Even plankton join in, oh who knew?

Every splash is a silly joke,
As squids squirt ink, watch the waves choke!
With a wink and a swirl, they play their part,
In this vibrant sea, it's a work of art.

Let's dive into fun; we'll party away,
With colors and laughter, oh what a play!
Join the currents, let's twirl and spin,
In the ocean of giggles, let the joy begin!

Aquatic Heartstrings

In the deep blue, a fishy band,
Playing tunes that are oh so grand.
A crab with a hat conducts with glee,
While sea cucumbers shimmy in the sea.

Tangled seaweed sings along,
With swirling lyrics, they can't go wrong.
Every rise and fall, a silly beat,
As dolphins twirl, they jump to their feet.

The anemones bounce with the sound,
As turtles tap dance all around.
With every chord, jellyfish sway,
In this underwater concert, let's play!

So grab your fins and join the throng,
In the rhythm of the waves, where we belong.
Come laugh and play in the sea so free,
Where hearts are light and spirits flee!

Currents of Reflection

Waves giggle and splash with glee,
Mirrors of mischief, wild and free.
Fish plan their pranks, with a flick and a flop,
As seagulls squawk tales, they just can't stop.

A starfish tells jokes, but no one will clap,
A crab rolling sideways caught in a trap.
The seaweed sways to a tune of its own,
While dolphins practice their latest dance drone.

Shells whisper secrets, soft as a sigh,
As silly sea cucumbers drift quietly by.
The tides make waves, but never with dread,
In this playful kingdom, all worries are shed.

Threads of Foam

Bubbles giggle, tickle toes,
Whimsical wisps as the breezy wind blows.
In frothy threads, the sea's tales unwind,
Where lost treasures dance, delightfully blind.

Lobsters wear glasses, feeling quite bold,
While jellyfish juggle and glow like gold.
Sandcastles tumble, what a grand sight,
As crabs cheer on their sandy delight.

A seal flips a fish, what a crafty jest,
While sea turtles stretch, they think they're the best.
With laughter and splashes, the waves play their part,
In this whimsical world, with a giggly heart.

Mirage on the Water

A shimmering dance on the surface so sly,
Pretending to hide, but it's all a big lie.
Mermaids gossip while brushing their hair,
While boisterous minnows dart here and there.

A whale cracked a joke, but lost its own tail,
As turtles in shades unhurriedly sail.
With each ripple, a giggle, a twist, and a twirl,
In the playground of water, life's a swirl.

Mysterious shapes float by with a grin,
Are they friends or mere tricks of the fin?
With laughter and light as the sun starts to gleam,
Reflections of joy dance in a dream.

The Call of the Abyss

Deep down below, where the wacky fish roam,
An octopus juggles in its watery home.
With eight silly arms, it makes quite a fuss,
While shadows of eels in the dark sit and cuss.

Bubbles bubble gossip, secrets of the deep,
As squids show off art in the dark, they leap.
With tales of adventure from shipwrecks and nets,
Creatures tell stories no human forgets.

A clam plays a harp with a glimmering shell,
While a pufferfish bursts out of its shell.
Under the waves, it's a comical spree,
Where everything's funny, just wait and see!

A Cauldron of Colors Beneath the Foam

Bubbles dance with laughter, oh so bright,
Fishes paint the water, a whimsical sight.
Seashells giggle in the sand, a funny bunch,
As crabs in tuxedos join the lunchtime crunch.

Starfish play hide and seek, oh what glee,
While jellyfish float like balloons, carefree.
An octopus juggles pearls with flair,
Winking at seagulls who just stop and stare.

The Ocean's Embrace and Echoes

Mermaids sing off-key, they're quite the crowd,
With seaweed hair and a giggly shroud.
Turtles race with a snail for a shell,
Who knew goldfish could dance so well?

Seagulls pluck snacks, thinking they're grand,
While dolphins tease, forming a band.
They play peek-a-boo with the rising tide,
As fish talk gossip, nowhere to hide.

Journey Through Liquid Light

A walrus wears sunglasses, soaking rays,
His beach ball bounces through crashing waves.
Crabs sporting shades strut across the shore,
While starry skies whisper, 'Just one more!'

The sandcastles giggle as they stand tall,
The tide rolls in, but they're having a ball.
Seahorses waltz through the dancing kelp,
While starfish ponder, 'What's this all about, help?'

Enigmas of the Deep Blue Serenade

Whales compose tunes that shake the sea,
They blow bubble notes, wild and free.
Anemones chuckle as they sway,
While clownfish perform in their own wacky play.

The grumpy angler fish turns on his light,
Revealing a party, oh what a sight!
An echolocation band, a symphonic treat,
As everyone joins in for a rhythmic beat.

Anemones' Caress

Jellyfish waltz with grace,
As crabs wear tiny hats.
Starfish cheer on the dance,
While seaweed plays like cats.

Turtles are the true DJs,
With shells that spin and glide.
Fish throw bubbles for beats,
Underwater they'll slide.

Colorful snails race fast,
But who can keep their shell?
Seahorses sing sea shanties,
In their own coral belle.

Anemones get a tickle,
As they burst out in giggles—
The party never stops,
In this place of sea wiggles.

Nostalgia in Sea Glass

In a bottle, tales are spun,
Whispers of the ocean wave.
Sea glass shines like memories,
From tides that misbehave.

Once a bottle, now a gem,
Collecting laughs and cheers.
The fragments chuckle with delight,
Of lost love and silly fears.

Sandcastles remind of times,
When life was pure and neat.
Tiny moats, grandiose dreams,
All washed up by retreat.

In these shards we find a laugh,
Of past and present fun.
Each piece tells a joke in hues,
Shining brightly in the sun.

Moonlit Reflections

Under stars, the waves clap hands,
With moonbeams joining the fun.
Silvery fish flash their smiles,
As night begins to run.

Crabs put on moonlight shows,
With their dancing, sidewise strut.
While dolphins tease with splashes,
In a sea of giggle and glut.

The water winks at the sky,
Like a friend sharing a joke.
As sea turtles laugh at clouds,
And bubbles rise like smoke.

So come, let's enjoy the show,
Where laughter floats and flies.
For in this gleaming moment,
The ocean sings with sighs.

Waters of Wonder

Where the gurgles meet the swells,
A dance of fish begins—
Octopuses juggle pearls,
While seagulls do their spins.

Waves toss around old shoes,
That washed up with a tale.
Mermaids giggle, pulling pranks,
As they waltz through the gale.

Sand dollars play hide-and-seek,
In the shimmering foam.
Crabs with bowties scuttle by,
In this playful, salty home.

Here in these fun waters,
The adventures never end.
So grab your floaty, join the jest,
And let the laughter blend.

Crystal Visions in Nautical Veils

Bubbles rise like tiny dreams,
Fish wear hats, or so it seems.
The crab's prance is quite a sight,
Dancing under disco light.

Mermaids giggle, splash around,
Their laughter echoes, quite profound.
An octopus, with flair, it twirls,
Inky plans, it's off to swirl.

Seashells whisper silly tales,
Of turtle races, wind, and sails.
Bright sea stars throw a party grand,
While seaweed stretches, makes a band.

Whales harmonize a joyful tune,
While clams dream of the next full moon.
With waves that tickle all in sight,
Under the sun's warm, golden light.

Harmony Among the Marine Realm

Crabs in leisure wiggle along,
While seahorses hum a cheery song.
Starfish try to start a band,
But they need a bit more hand.

A dolphin tells a joke so bright,
And plankton giggle in delight.
An eel twists in laugh-out-loud,
While fish gather, feeling proud.

Coral castles made of dreams,
Look like candy, or so it seems.
A puffer fish, quite round and fun,
Has jokes to share with everyone.

With each wave, a new story spins,
The sea's a place where laughter wins.
Beneath the waves, it's quite a scene,
Where every creature's happy and keen.

The Pulse of the Sea's Heartbeat

The surf floats in like giggly foam,
Where every fish can feel at home.
Crab races make the shells all cheer,
With silly grins as they appear.

A jellyfish spins with flair and grace,
While clownfish clown, keeping the pace.
Sea turtles wear their timepiece grand,
Awaiting the next sassy band.

The tides hum funny ocean tunes,
As seagulls chat about their spoons.
A shrimp sings scales with lots of flair,
And bubble parties fill the air.

With jellybeans from sailors' past,
Fish throw a shindig, surely a blast.
Each wave a giggle, each splash a cheer,
Amidst the sea, there's laughter near.

Mysteries Wrapped in Salty Stories

Beneath the waves, a tale untold,
Of wily sharks with hearts of gold.
A treasure map, a crab's new scheme,
Sailing forth on a crazy dream.

Seagulls squawk in comic tones,
While fishes share their phone-like moans.
Clams will argue, won't agree,
What's the best shade of kelp green sea.

With pearls that giggle in the sand,
And mermaids playing their flute band.
Whale whispers secrets from the deep,
While starfish prefer their beauty sleep.

A pirate's hat, with tales to share,
Brings laughter floating in the air.
In this salty world, every sprite,
Finds joy and giggles day and night.

Chasing Shadows in Moonlit Shallows

In the night, shadows dance,
Trying to give the moon a chance.
Fish in tuxedos swim with flair,
While big crabs pretend to care.

Glowworms giggle, lighting the way,
The silly shrimps just want to play.
Starfish waltz with grace so fine,
While jellyfish scribble love notes in brine.

Laughter bubbles from beneath the tide,
With octopuses dressed up, full of pride.
Seahorses prance in a silly race,
In this merry underwater space.

Tidal waves tickle each little fin,
As sea cucumbers grin and spin,
Every splash tells a joke so grand,
In this whimsical, watery land.

The Siren's Song of Tranquility

Siren whispers, quite absurd,
Humming tunes that sound like birds.
But her notes, a funny twist,
Turned all the dolphins into mist.

Seagulls giggle, rolling their eyes,
At the mermaid's silly lullabies.
Clownfish chuckle, in bubbles they float,
While starlets dream of rocking a boat.

Turtles nod to the rhythmic wave,
Chasing crabs that misbehave.
A sea sponge sings with unmatched glee,
While snails slow dance in jubilee.

Harmony reigns in a humorous way,
Even jellyfish learn to sway.
The dance of laughter on the tide,
Makes the sea a joyful ride.

Currents of Reflection and Reverie

Reflecting on life, what a show,
As waves crash quietly, fast and slow.
A fish looks in, expecting a star,
But finds just seaweed and a near-empty jar.

Clownfish crack jokes, they're quite divine,
Fiddler crabs holding a punchline line.
Underwater mirrors, full of blunders,
Laughter bubbles up in endless wonders.

Octopuses juggling, they slip and fall,
While turtles cheer, having a ball.
Unicorn fish blowing bubbles with glee,
In the current, they frolic so free.

Here in this watery world we glide,
Our troubles drift away with the tide.
A sea of giggles in the marine weave,
Life's funny moments, never to leave.

Aqua Dreams in Twilight's Glow

In twilight's glow, dreams come alive,
Where minnows in pajamas twist and dive.
Eels wear hats, much to our delight,
While wave crabs hold a fashion fight.

Dolphins trade stories, oh what a laugh,
About surfing the waves, it's a fun autograph.
Lobsters fool in a playful parade,
While snails compete in a slow charade.

Sardines sing softly, just off-key,
Their serenades make the corals giggle with glee.
Mussels clap shells in a rhythmic cheer,
As sea urchins chuckle without any fear.

With every ripple, another jest,
In this watery world, we are truly blessed.
Memories shimmer like stars in our souls,
Bathing in laughter, where humor consoles.

Celestial Waters

Bubbles rise, fish wear hats,
Crabs dance crazy, how about that?
Octopus juggling, quite a sight,
Seaweed wiggles, all in delight.

Waves are giggling, sun in a splash,
Starfish laugh, a colorful clash.
Dolphins play tag, with a flip and a twirl,
Shells whisper secrets, as they swirl.

Triton's Serenade

Triton sings in a bubbly tone,
With eels as backup, he's never alone.
Clams clap shells, keeping the beat,
While seahorses slide on their slippery feet.

Mermen've got jokes, they're quite the crowd,
Tales of treasure buried, they boast loud.
Mermaids chuckle, sharp as a dart,
Underwater romance, a comical art.

Reflections in the Deep

Fish in mirrors, they check their scales,
Pufferfish yolks, it's all fishy tales.
A grand parade of snorkelers swim,
With lost fins, their chances look grim.

Coral reefs whisper, "Don't take the bait,"
As jellyfish float, feeling first-rate.
A school of clownfish, they play their part,
Making puns before they depart.

Sirens of the Sapphire Sea

Sirens laugh, with shells on their ear,
Playing pranks that bring good cheer.
With tangled seaweed, they try to tease,
But fish just giggle and swim with ease.

Sapphire waves, they wiggle and sway,
Crabs on scooters, oh what a display!
Whales join in with deep, booming notes,
It's a party, where mermaids wear coats!

Luminous Currents

In waters bright, where fish do play,
A jellyfish floats by, a jiggly ballet.
Seagulls squawk, with wacky flair,
They squabble over snacks like they just don't care.

A clam tries to catch a passing wave,
But ends up stuck, feeling quite brave.
With every splash, it flops and spins,
Wondering if it's lost all its fins.

Starfish sit, in goofy glee,
Holding hands, oh silly sea!
They flip and flounder, not a care in sight,
For tides of laughter, oh what a sight!

As dolphins dance in a jovial race,
They splash about, each with a face.
The sea is a stage where giggles abound,
In every wave, pure joy is found.

Dance of the Tidepools

In tidepools deep, where critters reside,
A crab takes a polka with joy and pride.
A sea cucumber slips on its own slimy toes,
While anemones wave with their colorful clothes.

A shrimp tried to dance but jumped right out,
Landing on shore, with a surprised shout.
The starfish chuckled, an invertebrate tease,
As the shrimp found his groove with wobbly ease.

Mussels and clams form a conga line,
While barnacles groan, "Not this again, fine!"
With barnacles stuck, they can't get a break,
While others just giggle, for goodness' sake!

Through splashes and snorts, the tidepools sway,
In a whimsical dance, they laugh through the day.
With each silly step, beneath the sun's glow,
The tidepools unite in a comical show!

Beneath the Veil of Blue

Under waves where the funny fish roam,
A pufferfish pouts, "I miss my old home!"
With cheeks all puffed, it tries to look grand,
But bumps into friends like it's out of planned.

A quirky old turtle joins in the fun,
With flippers flapping, it gets on the run.
A disco of bubbles from lungs that are tight,
Causing fish nearby to bubble with fright!

A reef shark zips past with quite the dash,
Accidentally snags a kelp swirl, oh what a clash!
"Sorry," it mumbles, swimming away fast,
Leaving laughter behind as it fades in the vast.

With dolphins leaping and singing a tune,
The sea's great humor makes daytime feel like noon.
In a world of bright blues and playful delight,
Even fish can't help but giggle with might!

Frosted Waves

In winter's grip, the waves grow thick,
Where penguins slide, not a care they pick.
They wobble and tumble, such silly sights,
Waddling laughers in snowy delights.

A seal on a rock is sunbathing proud,
Till a wave comes a-knocking, "Oh no, I'm not cowed!"
It rolls with laughter, splatting around,
Turning a noble pose upside down!

A snow crab wearing a hat made of ice,
Thinks it's a fashion for crabs, oh how nice!
But gusts of wind twist it to and fro,
Leaving all crabs in a fit of woe.

Yet amidst frosted waves, joy always reigns,
For laughter flows freely through snowy domains.
With all of the sea creatures feeling the cheer,
They dance through the cold with abandon, oh dear!

The Rhythm of Raindrops

Raindrops dance on a tin roof,
Making music, oh so goof!
Puddles form like tiny pools,
Claiming space like water fools.

Worms wear hats, they swim with flair,
Jumping jigs without a care.
Frogs croak out a silly tune,
While fishes splash beneath the moon.

Ducks parade in stylish rows,
Waddling fast in funny clothes.
As clouds giggle with a rush,
Creating storms, oh what a fuss!

Splashing 'round, we join the play,
Laughing loud, come what may.
The world is wet but filled with cheer,
A raucous joy, we hold so dear.

Spectral Shores

Seagulls squawk in mismatched pairs,
Trying on their aviator wears.
Sandy toes and beach ball fights,
Laughter echoes, pure delights.

Crabs with buckets peek around,
Digging treasures in the ground.
"Hey, that's mine!" they shout with glee,
While chasing waves like comical bees.

Shells all giggle, cracking jokes,
As the tide rolls, funny folks.
Surfboards topple, splashes fly,
Superman's just a surfer guy!

At twilight, jokesters gather 'round,
Telling tales where fun abounds.
The night breaks with a sparkle bright,
Stealing smiles from day to night.

Charmed by the Current

Fish in hats swim with style,
Making waves as they beguile.
Jellybeans float, a candy spree,
Holding court in their jelly sea.

Bubbles burst with laughter's sound,
As seaweed dances all around.
Crabs in line for a sassy stroll,
Playing leapfrog, on a roll!

Starfish claim the disco floor,
Grooving hard, they shout for more.
"Spin me 'round," they laugh in glee,
The ocean's club, oh, let it be!

Turtles speeding, racing fate,
Slinking slow, oh isn't it great?
In this world of watery cheer,
Every splash draws friends near.

Fluid Dreams

In the waves, the dreamers drift,
Carried by currents, a happy gift.
Fish wearing glasses, reading books,
Crafting tales with quirky hooks.

An octopus in pajamas laughs,
Throwing jokes like silly crafts.
Seashells trade their best one-liners,
As dolphins dive, they're true diviners.

Silvery waves whisper soft charms,
While clam shells hold the sweetest farms.
In this dream where giggles gleam,
Reality is just a stream.

So let's float on this fluid scheme,
Laughter stitching through the seam.
With every wave, a new delight,
In watery dreams that last all night.

Breath of Celestial Currents

Bubbles rise with a joyful pop,
Fish wear goggles, they just can't stop.
A crab with a hat, quite the sight,
Dancing to waves under the moonlight.

Seaweed sways, what a wild dance,
Starfish claps, giving it a chance.
Gulls chuckle from their lofty throne,
Even the sea turtles drop their phones!

The jellyfish jiggles with glee,
While the octopus takes selfies.
Splashing fun from clamshells bright,
Underwater antics, sheer delight.

Whales sing songs, sonorous and deep,
Making the fish stick to their sleep.
Barnacles laugh, what a crazy scene,
Who knew the sea could be so mean?

Ebbing Echoes

Waves attend a comedy show,
Tide pulls back, but won't let go.
Clams crack jokes on sandy stages,
While dolphins write their funny pages.

Seahorses trot in fashionable flair,
Flipping their tails without a care.
A pufferfish wears a polka dot,
Spreading laughter, tying the knot!

The tide rolls in on a rubber raft,
Everyone's giggling, what a draft!
Anemones dance, waving their arms,
Flirting with fish, sharing their charms.

The sandcastle stands, a royal court,
Crushed by a wave, it's an all-time sport.
Shells debt collectors, the corals sigh,
In this caper, laughter won't die!

Tides of Transparency

Clear waters reveal a fishy game,
Where anchovies play hide-and-seek, oh, lame!
A clam playing poker under a rock,
Each time it wins, it lets out a squawk!

The sea cucumbers strut and boast,
"Who has more bling?" says one with a toast.
Crabs gossip under a kelp tree,
All while the dolphins giggle with glee.

Starfish claim they're the best at art,
Painting the sand with a little heart.
Pufferfish pose for their close-up scene,
With shells and pearls lined up pristine.

Turtles racing, a comical chase,
Belly flops turn into a graceful grace.
Giggling sea urchins, dressed in bling,
Under these tides, what joy we bring!

Secrets Beneath the Surface

Beneath the waves, a secret club,
Where fish gossip and giggle, oh hub!
A sea otter teaches the latest dance,
Whirl and twirl, it's a watery trance.

Nudibranchs flaunt their colors bright,
While snails race in a slow-motion fight.
Lobsters know where the best snacks are,
Bartering shells like they're a star.

Crabs wear tiaras, feeling elite,
Seducing seaweed with a funky beat.
Octopuses hide in the laughter whirl,
What a world beneath that swirly curl!

With every splash, a new prank unfolds,
Mermaids giggling, they're breaking the molds.
Underwater fun, secrets that gleam,
In this party, we all swim and dream!

Whispers from the Coral Gardens

Bubbles giggle as they rise,
Coral fish wear silly ties.
A starfish jokes with seaweed scenes,
As jellybeans swim in gleams.

Seahorses dance in clumsy spins,
While crabs argue about their sins.
Anemones wave like crazy flags,
While clownfish boast of all their jags.

Up above, the sun's a clown,
Making shadows dance up and down.
The octopus plays hide and seek,
With a clam that can't help but squeak.

In gardens where the shells all sing,
A hermit crab finds the silliest bling.
They laugh at tides that splush and splash,
In oceans full of sparkly trash.

Sapphire Embrace

A dolphin wears a rainbow cap,
While sea turtles take a nap.
The waves are ticklish, full of cheer,
As fish parade in laughter near.

A blue whale sings a silly tune,
While crabs crabwalk under the moon.
Stingrays glide with graceful flair,
Tickling sea urchins unaware.

Funny shrimps jump with delight,
As seagulls swoop in a playful flight.
An old shipwreck chuckles too,
While barnacles laugh and feel brand new.

In this embrace of vibrant hues,
Jellyfish jiggle in funny shoes.
The sapphire waves cling and tease,
Making everyone laugh with ease.

Crystal Cascades

Water drips like melted cheese,
A fish rides in on a gentle breeze.
Urchins giggle, tickling sand,
With hermit crabs offering a hand.

The sound of splashes brings a grin,
As sardines rush to join the din.
Pufferfish puff, their cheeks expand,
Creating bubbles that form a band.

Oh what fun as rainbows fly,
With sea cows dancing, oh my, oh my!
A treasure chest full of clownish dreams,
Where each pearl bursts with laughter beams.

In cascades bright with crystal light,
The sea plays tricks, oh what a sight!
With every splash and giggle shared,
The ocean's fun crew is well-prepared.

Glimmering Horizons

The sun gets shy, a golden cue,
While fish in shades of every hue.
Splashing joy, they leap and twirl,
As dolphins prank in a water swirl.

Starfish dance on their pointy toes,
While a grouper tries on mismatched clothes.
The horizon laughs, it can't resist,
As waves burst up in glittery mist.

Pelicans stumble on their flight,
While seahorses play peek-a-boo at night.
The moon joins in with a smile so wide,
As shells hold secrets of the ocean's pride.

In this place where silliness reigns,
Laughter echoes through watery lanes.
Life's a party, bright and bold,
In glimmering waves, tales are told.

Enigmas of the Tide

A jellyfish waltzes, all gooey and bright,
With its dance moves, it gives quite a fright.
A crab in a tux, oh what a fine sight,
In a shell-made car, it zooms left and right.

The waves play their games, roll in with a laugh,
While seagulls drop popcorn, what a funny gaffe!
A fish wearing glasses, quite the sleek staff,
Says, "Life's just a splash, don't forget to do math!"

There's treasure beneath where the flippers flop,
A sock from a pirate? It makes the heart stop!
"Who needs gold doubloons? Just give me a mop!"
As laughter erupts from the sand and the crop.

So come join the frolics, take off your shoes,
Let's mingle with mermaids, learn all their views.
For in tidal waters, there's never bad news,
Just bubbles and giggles, and jellybean chews.

Refraction of Light

A dolphin in shades, what a cool dude!
Sliding on waves, he's prime party food.
He flips through the sunlight, so spry and so shrewd,
Telling jokes at the reef, oh! This ocean's a brood.

With seabed disco, all creatures unite,
The squids glow in colors – oh, what a sight!
An octopus DJ spins tunes day and night,
While krill dance in swarms, a synchronized rite.

In this puzzling prism where shadows play tricks,
A clam tells a joke, and it gets quite a fix.
"Why don't we ever play musical licks?"
"Because someone might get pinned with a flick!"

Underwater laughter, we do a light jig,
Boogie with bubbles, let's all dance big.
The stories we concoct, they really are big,
When the clams and the fish make us all feel like kings.

Chasing Sapphire Shadows

A turtle named Timmy broke into a sprint,
But tripped on a seaweed – oh, what a hint!
The starfish all giggled, "Look at that glint!"
As he rolled in the sand, they clapped in delight.

The seahorses racing, neck-and-neck, what a sight,
One forgot the way, darting left in its flight.
"Hey buddy, wrong turn!" they chuckled in spite,
Leading the way, they laughed through the night.

A treasure map drawn with sandwich designs,
Those curious fish, well, they thought it was fines.
"Let's find the 'Lunch', it's about that time,"
Said a clownfish dressed up, with bright colored lines.

With bubbles a-popping, they all formed a crew,
In search of the feast, the fabled fish stew.
In the realm of the waves, there's laughter anew,
In conversing with shadows, their friendship just grew.

Wind's Whisper

The wind tells a tale, with a chuckle so spry,
Of mermaids who giggle as clouds drift by.
Meanwhile, a shrimp is busy baking a pie,
That smells like the ocean with a twist of the sky.

A seagull swoops down, hoping just for a taste,
But rivals the clam who won't share, what a waste!
They argue for ages, without any haste,
While fish pass the popcorn, just keeping it chaste.

Here the tides do their jig, with bubbles in tow,
While tadpoles recall tales of journeys below.
"Have you seen that big wave? It steals all the show!"
They giggle and wiggle, nature's own glow.

So come feel the breeze, let it tickle your cheek,
Participate in the fun, the laughs we do seek.
For in this watery land, silliness peaks,
Dive deep into joy, let the vibrant tide speak.

Whispers of Deep Blue Wonder

Bubbles rise, fish have a chat,
Octopus dances with a top hat.
Seagulls giggle, making a fuss,
They're plotting to steal your lunch—how rude of us!

Mermaids sing their songs with glee,
But watch out, they're eyeing your PB&J.
Crabs wear shades, strutting on sand,
While dolphins plan a rock band tour, oh so grand!

Starfish throw a beach party tonight,
With jellyfish spinning under moonlight.
The tide's the DJ, making waves swell,
As sardines dance like they know swell!

So grab your towel, join in the fun,
In this watery world, life's a splashy run!
Just watch your snacks, and take a seat,
For the ocean's giggles can't be beat!

Secrets Beneath the Tides

Clams hold tales of ages gone by,
While sea turtles whisper, 'Give it a try!'
Jellyfish juggle, oh what a sight,
As they float along with no sense of fright.

Barnacles gossip, stuck to their rocks,
Plotting their moves like well-timed clocks.
Shrimps wear tuxedos, all dressed to impress,
While octopuses argue—just a friendly mess!

In this deep blue circus, no one feels shy,
A crab with a monocle gives fashion a try.
Seahorses prance in their tiny parade,
While fish trade secrets, in this cool charade.

So dive in the laughter, swim with delight,
In the depths of the sea, it's a hilarious sight!
Mermaids wink and the whales sing along,
Together they make the ocean's own song!

Reflections in the Celestial Waters

Stars above wink at fish moving fast,
While the moon tells tales of the tide's steadfast.
A pelican grins, about to make a splash,
As he dives for his dinner, not just a dash!

Ducks wear capes and swim with style,
While seahorses twirl, making us smile.
Fish in bow ties take the floor,
In this underwater ballroom, who could ask for more?

Coral reefs giggle, dressed to the nines,
With colors so bright, they hold fancy lines.
A starfish grumps, 'Why am I stuck here?'
But the seaweed says, 'Chill, it's party, my dear!'

So come join the fun in this sparkling abode,
Where the moonlight dances on a wavy road.
With laughter and joy, we'll sail through the night,
In these whimsical waters, everything's bright!

Embrace of the Sapphire Waves

Splashing about, the sea's full of jest,
Where sea cucumbers think they're the best.
Waves crash and giggle, tickling your toes,
As playful dolphins put on a show.

Fish flip and flop, what a silly scene,
While sandcastles tremble, but they're not mean.
Crustaceans kick back with lemonade cups,
While the seaweed dances, never gives up!

Whales tell jokes while swimming in sync,
Their laughter is loud, just stop and think.
As the tide rolls in, life makes a fuss,
Even the sea anemone joins the bus!

So grab your floaties, let's ride the spree,
In the embrace of waves, wild and free.
For laughter blooms bright in the ocean's sway,
In this sapphire realm, come join the play!

Luminous Depths: A Love Letter

In the depths where fish do dance,
I swear I saw a starfish prance!
With sunglasses on, it flashed a smile,
And then it vanished—what a style!

The crabs held court with tiny crowns,
While jellyfish floated wearing gowns.
I wish to dive, to join this crew,
But seasick thoughts might chase me, too!

A dolphin winked, said, "Take a chance!"
As bubbles popped in silly dance.
With laughter echoing through the blue,
I'd swim forever, just me and you!

Oh, treasure chests may hold the gold,
But a dancing fish is worth more than told.
In this whimsical, watery affair,
My heart's afloat—there's love in the air!

Tidal Tales of Enchantment

The waves rolled in with a giggle and splash,
Caught me off guard, a bubbly crash!
I slipped on sand, with grace I fell,
The seagulls laughed—oh, can't you tell?

Seashells whispered secrets so bright,
Of mermaids who don't quite take flight.
They trip on fins and lose their combs,
Wishing all day they had seafoam homes!

Crabs recite poetry upon the shore,
One chef even tried to start a war.
He served up sushi, they felt betrayed,
"Keep your pinchers—this is a parade!"

The tide is high but spirits are higher,
Each splash and wave, a dance of desire.
With laughter and light, let's make a toast,
To watery tales we'll always boast!

Resonance of the Sea's True Essence

The ocean sings in tones so bright,
With dolphins practicing day and night.
A beluga solo—it's quite the feat,
But doesn't quite match my tapping feet!

Buckets of crabs joined in the show,
Doing a jig, putting on a glow.
Between the waves, a seaweed band,
With clams as tambourines, oh what a stand!

They held a rock concert on a boat,
Surfboards becoming their favorite coat.
The starfish crowd cheered with glee,
As the barnacles danced—such a sight to see!

I joined the fun, played a seashell horn,
With laughter twinkling like the morn.
An oceanic symphony, oh so wild,
Where even sea monsters laughed like a child!

Serenity's Ripple in Solitude

A quiet tide where seagulls roam,
With soft, sandy dunes—my heart feels home.
I raised my arms to the warm sunlight,
Only to trip, what a clumsy sight!

The hermit crabs chuckled and wheeled,
As I stumbled on their sandy field.
"Don't take it hard, we all have our days!"
They'll surely charge me for laughter pays!

Waves lapped gently, like whispers sweet,
But in that moment, I took my seat.
A sandcastle king might've just arrived,
But all he did was hide and thrive!

So here's to the bliss found in this mess,
With a splash and a fall, oh what a quest!
Laughter and solitude hand in hand,
In this silly realm of driftwood land!

Sonatas of Soft Sand

Seashells are chairs for the crabs,
They wiggle and dance like happy little jabs.
The tide rolls in, a sly little thief,
Stealing my sandwich, oh what a relief!

Sandcastles rise, then tumble down,
Moats don't work when you're still in town.
A seagull swoops with a cheeky caw,
And steals my chips with a beak full of law.

Oh, to swim in waves of bubbly delight,
With seaweed wigs, what a comical sight!
Mermaids laugh, they know the truth,
In tepid water, one loses their youth!

So let's twist and twirl in sandy retreats,
With polka-dot shorts and mismatched tweets.
The shoreline beckons with a playful tone,
And here I sit, my throne made of foam.

Rhapsody of Seaweed

Underwater forests swaying in glee,
A fish in a tux, sipping herbal tea.
The seaweed sings, oh what a tune,
While shrimp do a jig beneath the pale moon.

Crabs wear sunglasses, strutting so proud,
While jellyfish float like a fanciful cloud.
A whale sings bass in a melodic groove,
In this ballet of bubbles, we all must move!

Sand dollars gossip, they chat and they cling,
About that one starfish who danced like a king.
The current's just laughter, a tickle on skin,
As I dive below, let the fun begin!

Oh, the symphony plays in the swell,
With fish playing maracas, oh what a spell!
In the depths of the blue, let our spirits rewind,
To the rhapsody sung by the whimsical kind.

Ephemeral Tides

The tides roll in with a goofy grin,
Waves crashing loudly, let the fun begin!
Seashells are treasures, but they're hard to find,
With a pocketful of sand, I'm still feeling fine.

Floating on floats, what a silly sight,
As dolphins unite in a splashy fight.
I paddle my boat with a chicken-like flap,
While kids in the sand keep falling with a clap!

Laughter resounds, a melody sweet,
As seagulls patrol for my lunch to eat.
In a race with the tide, I'm out of breath,
I wave to the waves, oh sweet dance of death!

Each splash a giggle, each foam a cheer,
This world of whimsy, oh how we revere!
As the sun dips low, let's frolic and glide,
For these fleeting moments, let joy be our guide.

Swirls of Tranquility

In a whirl of colors, the beach starts to sway,
As sand tickles toes in a cheeky ballet.
With flip-flops flapping, we jog to the surf,
Squealing with joy, like we're back on this Earth!

Fish flip like acrobats just for a show,
While barnacles gossip about that one crow.
The tide winks at me, with bubbles in tow,
Crafting portraits in foam, oh what a flow!

Laughter echoes, it's echoed by crabs,
While beach balls bounce like topsy-turvy jabs.
The sand drops a wink, I give it a cheer,
For swirling in fun is the best souvenir!

So let's twirl and giggle, under skies so blue,
With floaties and laughter, there's much we can do.
In this world of waves, let your spirit fly,
For serenity's swirls make us feel like we're high!

Echoes of the Brine

In the splash of the wave, I see a smile,
A fishy grin from a bass, quite the style.
They giggle and wiggle as I walk by,
Who knew gills could jest? Oh my, oh my!

The crabs throw a party, they're quite the beat,
Tap dancing sideways, they move their feet.
A seagull swoops down, steals a crab's snack,
The crustacean cries out, "Hey, that's a whack!"

A dolphin does flips, showing off in the sun,
While I bask on the sand, pouring out some fun.
With shells that can sing and seaweed that dances,
I ponder the ocean's whimsical glances.

But just when I'm lost in the laughter and cheer,
A wave comes a-knocking, "Hey, come swim here!"
Instead of a splash, it's more like a dunk,
"Who knew the tide could also be punk?"

Mysteries in Aquamarine

Beneath the waves hides a treasure trove,
Where mermaids play hide-and-seek as they strove.
Their giggles echo, like bubbles in flight,
Swapping tales with fish, what a silly sight!

An octopus juggles, with arms all aglow,
While a clam claps slowly, putting on a show.
A starfish plays maracas, but it can't quite sing,
It winks and it blinks, it's a funky thing!

The turtles come along, moving oh so slow,
"Let's have a race!" they declare, full of glow.
But who's supposed to win? It's quite the debate,
As they munch on seaweed and contemplate fate.

But just when I think it's a joyous affair,
A wave crashes down, splashing everywhere.
I laugh as I tumble, embraced by the sea,
Even the jellyfish giggles with glee!

Embrace of the Deep

In the depths of blue, there's a wacky scene,
A seahorse doing yoga, looking quite serene.
Anemones cheer, waving their frilly arms,
"Breathe in that salt air, feel the ocean charms!"

A shark with a visor, oh what a sight!
Says, "I'm just here for the vibe, not the bite!"
While fish form a band, they're playing a tune,
As rays dance around, twinkling like the moon.

Clam shells are clapping to the underwater beat,
With algae doing pirouettes on dainty feet.
"Join us!" they call, but I'm in too deep,
For every time I jump, I just make a heap!

But laughter erupts, even when I slip,
Each splash is a chuckle, not a sinking ship.
In the embrace of the deep, life's nothing but glee,
With friends made of sand, and tales of the sea!

Tidal Reverie

As I stroll on the shore with my toes in the wet,
I spot a crab wearing a tiny sun hat.
It waves as it scuttles, a sight so absurd,
Who knew crustaceans had style undeterred?

The waves come tumbling, a bubbly parade,
With sea foam confetti, they've got it made.
And the shells all giggle, on this sandy stage,
As I dance along, feeling carefree and sage.

A seal pops its head up, with a wink and a grin,
"Want to join our splash fest? Come on in!"
But just as I leap, the tide pulls me back,
"Oh no!" I cry out, "This water's a hack!"

Yet amidst the splashes and charming chaos,
The ocean just chuckles, and I take a pause.
In this tidal reverie, laughter's the art,
For every wave whispers, "Joy is the start!"